2019

This Planner Belongs To -

....

....

....

....

2019

January
S	M	T	W	T	F	S
		1	2	3	4	5
6	7	8	9	10	11	12
13	14	15	16	17	18	19
20	21	22	23	24	25	26
27	28	29	30	31		

February
S	M	T	W	T	F	S
					1	2
3	4	5	6	7	8	9
10	11	12	13	14	15	16
17	18	19	20	21	22	23
24	25	26	27	28		

March
S	M	T	W	T	F	S
					1	2
3	4	5	6	7	8	9
10	11	12	13	14	15	16
17	18	19	20	21	22	23
24	25	26	27	28	29	30
31						

April
S	M	T	W	T	F	S
	1	2	3	4	5	6
7	8	9	10	11	12	13
14	15	16	17	18	19	20
21	22	23	24	25	26	27
28	29	30				

May
S	M	T	W	T	F	S
			1	2	3	4
5	6	7	8	9	10	11
12	13	14	15	16	17	18
19	20	21	22	23	24	25
26	27	28	29	30	31	

June
S	M	T	W	T	F	S
						1
2	3	4	5	6	7	8
9	10	11	12	13	14	15
16	17	18	19	20	21	22
23	24	25	26	27	28	29
30						

July
S	M	T	W	T	F	S
	1	2	3	4	5	6
7	8	9	10	11	12	13
14	15	16	17	18	19	20
21	22	23	24	25	26	27
28	29	30	31			

July
S	M	T	W	T	F	S
	1	2	3	4	5	6
7	8	9	10	11	12	13
14	15	16	17	18	19	20
21	22	23	24	25	26	27
28	29	30	31			

September
S	M	T	W	T	F	S
1	2	3	4	5	6	7
8	9	10	11	12	13	14
15	16	17	18	19	20	21
22	23	24	25	26	27	28
29	30					

October
S	M	T	W	T	F	S
		1	2	3	4	5
6	7	8	9	10	11	12
13	14	15	16	17	18	19
20	21	22	23	24	25	26
27	28	29	30	31		

November
S	M	T	W	T	F	S
					1	2
3	4	5	6	7	8	9
10	11	12	13	14	15	16
17	18	19	20	21	22	23
24	25	26	27	28	29	30

December
S	M	T	W	T	F	S
1	2	3	4	5	6	7
8	9	10	11	12	13	14
15	16	17	18	19	20	21
22	23	24	25	26	27	28
29	30	31				

Goals for 2019

"Our greatest glory is not in never falling but in rising every time we fall"

Confuscius

December

Week 1   12/31/18 to 01/06/19

○ 31. MONDAY

PRIORITIES

○ 1. TUESDAY

○ 2. WEDNESDAY

TO DO

○ 3. THURSDAY

○ 4. FRIDAY

○ 5. SATURDAY / 6. SUNDAY

"The secret of getting ahead is getting started"
Mark Twain

January

Week 2   01/07/19 to 01/13/19

○ 7. MONDAY

PRIORITIES

○ 8. TUESDAY

○ 9. WEDNESDAY

TO DO

○ 10. THURSDAY

○ 11. FRIDAY

○ 12. SATURDAY / 13. SUNDAY

If your actions inspire others to dream more, learn more, do more and become more, you are a leader. ~ John Quincy Adams, American former president from 1825 to 1829

January

Week 3   01/14/19 to 01/20/19

○ 14. MONDAY   PRIORITIES

○ 15. TUESDAY

○ 16. WEDNESDAY
                                        TO DO

○ 17. THURSDAY

○ 18. FRIDAY

○ 19. SATURDAY / 20. SUNDAY

Do not dwell in the past, do not dream of the future, concentrate the mind on the present moment. ~ Gautama Buddha

January

Week 4   01/21/19 to 01/27/19

○ 21. MONDAY

                                              PRIORITIES

○ 22. TUESDAY

○ 23. WEDNESDAY

                                              TO DO

○ 24. THURSDAY

○ 25. FRIDAY

○ 26. SATURDAY / 27. SUNDAY

For success, attitude is equally as important as ability.
~ Walter Scott, Scottish novelist and poet, 1771-1832

January

Week 5   01/28/19 to 02/03/19

○ 28. MONDAY

PRIORITIES

○ 29. TUESDAY

○ 30. WEDNESDAY

TO DO

○ 31. THURSDAY

○ 1. FRIDAY

○ 2. SATURDAY / 3. SUNDAY

There are only two mistakes one can make along the road to truth: Not going all the way, and not starting.
~ Gautama Buddha

February

Week 6   02/04/19 to 02/10/19

○ 4. MONDAY

                                 PRIORITIES

○ 5. TUESDAY

○ 6. WEDNESDAY

                                 TO DO

○ 7. THURSDAY

○ 8. FRIDAY

○ 9. SATURDAY / 10. SUNDAY

Wise men speak because they have something to say; Fools because they have to say something. ~ Plato, Ancient Greek philosopher

February

Week 7   02/11/19 to 02/17/19

○ 11. MONDAY

PRIORITIES

○ 12. TUESDAY

○ 13. WEDNESDAY

TO DO

○ 14. THURSDAY

○ 15. FRIDAY

○ 16. SATURDAY / 17. SUNDAY

Happiness is the only good. The time to be happy is now. The place to be happy is here. The way to be happy is to make others so ~ Robert Green Ingersoll

February

Week 8   02/18/19 to 02/24/19

○ 18. MONDAY

○ 19. TUESDAY

○ 20. WEDNESDAY

○ 21. THURSDAY

○ 22. FRIDAY

○ 23. SATURDAY / 24. SUNDAY

PRIORITIES

TO DO

We are shaped by our thoughts; we become what we think. ~ Gautama Buddha

March

Week 13   03/25/19 to 03/31/19

○ 25. MONDAY

PRIORITIES

○ 26. TUESDAY

○ 27. WEDNESDAY

TO DO

○ 28. THURSDAY

○ 29. FRIDAY

○ 30. SATURDAY / 31. SUNDAY

Knowing is not enough; we must apply. Willing is not enough; we must do. ~ Johann Wolfgang von Goethe, German writer and statesman, 1749- 1832

April

Week 14   04/01/19 to 04/07/19

○ 1. MONDAY

○ 2. TUESDAY

○ 3. WEDNESDAY

○ 4. THURSDAY

○ 5. FRIDAY

○ 6. SATURDAY / 7. SUNDAY

PRIORITIES

TO DO

Do not dwell in the past, do not dream of the future, concentrate the mind on the present moment. ~ Gautama Buddha

April

Week 15

04/08/19 to 04/14/19

○ 8. MONDAY

PRIORITIES

○ 9. TUESDAY

○ 10. WEDNESDAY

TO DO

○ 11. THURSDAY

○ 12. FRIDAY

○ 13. SATURDAY / 14. SUNDAY

Nothing can stop the man with the right mental attitude from achieving his goal; nothing on earth can help the man with the wrong mental attitude. ~ Thomas Jefferson, American former president from 1801 to 1809

April

Week 16

04/15/19 to 04/21/19

○ 15. MONDAY

○ 16. TUESDAY

○ 17. WEDNESDAY

○ 18. THURSDAY

○ 19. FRIDAY

○ 20. SATURDAY / 21. SUNDAY

PRIORITIES

TO DO

It is the mark of an educated mind to be able to entertain a thought without accepting it. ~ Aristotle, Ancient Greek philosopher

April

Week 17

04/22/19 to 04/28/19

○ 22. MONDAY

PRIORITIES

○ 23. TUESDAY

○ 24. WEDNESDAY

TO DO

○ 25. THURSDAY

○ 26. FRIDAY

○ 27. SATURDAY / 28. SUNDAY

True happiness is... to enjoy the present, without anxious dependence upon the future. ~ Lucius Annaeus Seneca, Roman philosopher

April

Week 18

04/29/19 to 05/05/19

○ 29. MONDAY

PRIORITIES

○ 30. TUESDAY

○ 1. WEDNESDAY

TO DO

○ 2. THURSDAY

○ 3. FRIDAY

○ 4. SATURDAY / 5. SUNDAY

As I grow older, I pay less attention to what men say. I just watch what they do. ~ Andrew Carnegie, Scottish businessman, 1835-1919

May

Week 19

05/06/19 to 05/12/19

○ 6. MONDAY

PRIORITIES

○ 7. TUESDAY

○ 8. WEDNESDAY

TO DO

○ 9. THURSDAY

○ 10. FRIDAY

○ 11. SATURDAY / 12. SUNDAY

Do not take life too seriously. You will never get out of it alive. ~ Elbert Hubbard, American writer, 1859-1915

May

Week 20

05/13/19 to 05/19/19

○ 13. MONDAY

PRIORITIES

○ 14. TUESDAY

○ 15. WEDNESDAY

TO DO

○ 16. THURSDAY

○ 17. FRIDAY

○ 18. SATURDAY / 19. SUNDAY

Positive anything is better than negative nothing. Elbert Hubbard, American writer, 1859-1915

May

Week 21   05/20/19 to 05/26/19

○ 20. MONDAY

○ 21. TUESDAY

○ 22. WEDNESDAY

○ 23. THURSDAY

○ 24. FRIDAY

○ 25. SATURDAY / 26. SUNDAY

PRIORITIES

TO DO

Don't judge each day by the harvest that you reap but by the seeds that you plant. Robert Louis Stevenson, Scottish poet and novelist

May
Week 22   05/27/19 to 06/02/19

○ 27. MONDAY

PRIORITIES

○ 28. TUESDAY

○ 29. WEDNESDAY

TO DO

○ 30. THURSDAY

○ 31. FRIDAY

○ 1. SATURDAY / 2. SUNDAY

To avoid criticism, do nothing, say nothing, and be nothing. Elbert Hubbard, American writer, 1859-1915

June

Week 23   06/03/19 to 06/09/19

○ 3. MONDAY

○ 4. TUESDAY

○ 5. WEDNESDAY

○ 6. THURSDAY

○ 7. FRIDAY

○ 8. SATURDAY / 9. SUNDAY

PRIORITIES

TO DO

To keep the body in good health is a duty ... otherwise we shall not be able to keep our mind strong and clear. ~ Gautama Buddha

June

Week 24

06/10/19 to 06/16/19

○ 10. MONDAY

PRIORITIES

○ 11. TUESDAY

○ 12. WEDNESDAY

TO DO

○ 13. THURSDAY

○ 14. FRIDAY

○ 15. SATURDAY / 16. SUNDAY

When words fail, music speaks
Shhakespeare

June

Week 25

06/17/19 to 06/23/19

O 17. MONDAY

PRIORITIES

O 18. TUESDAY

O 19. WEDNESDAY

TO DO

O 20. THURSDAY

O 21. FRIDAY

O 22. SATURDAY / 23. SUNDAY

There is no great genius without some form of madness
Aristotle

June

Week 26   06/24/19 to 06/30/19

○ 24. MONDAY

PRIORITIES

○ 25. TUESDAY

○ 26. WEDNESDAY

TO DO

○ 27. THURSDAY

○ 28. FRIDAY

○ 29. SATURDAY / 30. SUNDAY

Sometimes you put up walls not to keep others out. But to see who cares enough to knock them down.
Socrates

July

Week 27

07/01/19 to 07/07/19

○ 1. MONDAY

PRIORITIES

○ 2. TUESDAY

○ 3. WEDNESDAY

TO DO

○ 4. THURSDAY

○ 5. FRIDAY

○ 6. SATURDAY / 7. SUNDAY

"A room without books is like a body without a soul."
— **Marcus Tullius Cicero**

July
Week 28

07/08/19 to 07/14/19

○ 8. MONDAY

PRIORITIES

○ 9. TUESDAY

○ 10. WEDNESDAY

TO DO

○ 11. THURSDAY

○ 12. FRIDAY

○ 13. SATURDAY / 14. SUNDAY

"Be the change that you wish to see in the world."
— **Mahatma Gandhi**

July
Week 29   07/15/19 to 07/21/19

○ 15. MONDAY

PRIORITIES

○ 16. TUESDAY

○ 17. WEDNESDAY

TO DO

○ 18. THURSDAY

○ 19. FRIDAY

○ 20. SATURDAY / 21. SUNDAY

"If you tell the truth, you don't have to remember anything."
— **Mark Twain**

July

Week 30

07/22/19 to 07/28/19

○ 22. MONDAY

PRIORITIES

○ 23. TUESDAY

○ 24. WEDNESDAY

TO DO

○ 25. THURSDAY

○ 26. FRIDAY

○ 27. SATURDAY / 28. SUNDAY

"A friend is someone who knows all about you and still loves you."
— **Elbert Hubbard**

July
Week 31

07/29/19 to 08/04/19

○ 29. MONDAY

PRIORITIES

○ 30. TUESDAY

○ 31. WEDNESDAY

TO DO

○ 1. THURSDAY

○ 2. FRIDAY

○ 3. SATURDAY / 4. SUNDAY

"Always forgive your enemies; nothing annoys them so much."
— **Oscar Wilde**

August

Week 32   08/05/19 to 08/11/19

○ 5. MONDAY

○ 6. TUESDAY

○ 7. WEDNESDAY

○ 8. THURSDAY

○ 9. FRIDAY

○ 10. SATURDAY / 11. SUNDAY

PRIORITIES

TO DO

"Live as if you were to die tomorrow. Learn as if you were to live forever."
— **Mahatma Gandhi**

August

Week 33   08/12/19 to 08/18/19

○ 12. MONDAY

                                                PRIORITIES

○ 13. TUESDAY

○ 14. WEDNESDAY

                                                TO DO

○ 15. THURSDAY

○ 16. FRIDAY

○ 17. SATURDAY / 18. SUNDAY

"To live is the rarest thing in the world. Most people exist, that is all."
— **Oscar Wilde**

August

Week 34

08/19/19 to 08/25/19

○ 19. MONDAY

○ 20. TUESDAY

○ 21. WEDNESDAY

○ 22. THURSDAY

○ 23. FRIDAY

○ 24. SATURDAY / 25. SUNDAY

PRIORITIES

TO DO

"To be yourself in a world that is constantly trying to make you something else is the greatest accomplishment."
— **Ralph Waldo Emerson**

August
Week 35

08/26/19 to 09/01/19

○ 26. MONDAY

PRIORITIES

○ 27. TUESDAY

○ 28. WEDNESDAY

TO DO

○ 29. THURSDAY

○ 30. FRIDAY

○ 31. SATURDAY / 1. SUNDAY

"Without music, life would be a mistake."
— **Friedrich Nietzsche,**

September

Week 36

09/02/19 to 09/08/19

○ 2. MONDAY

○ 3. TUESDAY

○ 4. WEDNESDAY

○ 5. THURSDAY

○ 6. FRIDAY

○ 7. SATURDAY / 8. SUNDAY

PRIORITIES

TO DO

"There are only two ways to live your life. One is as though nothing is a miracle. The other is as though everything is a miracle."
— **Albert Einstein**

September

Week 37

09/09/19 to 09/15/19

○ 9. MONDAY

PRIORITIES

○ 10. TUESDAY

○ 11. WEDNESDAY

TO DO

○ 12. THURSDAY

○ 13. FRIDAY

○ 14. SATURDAY / 15. SUNDAY

"Good friends, good books, and a sleepy conscience: this is the ideal life."
— **Mark Twain**

September

Week 38

09/16/19 to 09/22/19

○ 16. MONDAY

○ 17. TUESDAY

○ 18. WEDNESDAY

○ 19. THURSDAY

○ 20. FRIDAY

○ 21. SATURDAY / 22. SUNDAY

PRIORITIES

TO DO

"The man who does not read has no advantage over the man who cannot read."
— **Mark Twain**

September

Week 39

09/23/19 to 09/29/19

○ 23. MONDAY

PRIORITIES

○ 24. TUESDAY

○ 25. WEDNESDAY

TO DO

○ 26. THURSDAY

○ 27. FRIDAY

○ 28. SATURDAY / 29. SUNDAY

"It is not a lack of love, but a lack of friendship that makes unhappy marriages."
— **Friedrich Nietzsche**

September

Week 40

09/30/19 to 10/06/19

○ 30. MONDAY

PRIORITIES

○ 1. TUESDAY

○ 2. WEDNESDAY

TO DO

○ 3. THURSDAY

○ 4. FRIDAY

○ 5. SATURDAY / 6. SUNDAY

"Love all, trust a few, do wrong to none."
— **William Shakespeare,**

October

Week 41   10/07/19 to 10/13/19

○ 7. MONDAY

                                                    PRIORITIES

○ 8. TUESDAY

○ 9. WEDNESDAY

                                                    TO DO

○ 10. THURSDAY

○ 11. FRIDAY

○ 12. SATURDAY / 13. SUNDAY

"Never put off till tomorrow what may be done day after tomorrow just as well."
— **Mark Twain**

October

Week 42   10/14/19 to 10/20/19

- ○ 14. MONDAY

PRIORITIES

- ○ 15. TUESDAY

- ○ 16. WEDNESDAY

TO DO

- ○ 17. THURSDAY

- ○ 18. FRIDAY

- ○ 19. SATURDAY / 20. SUNDAY

"That which does not kill us makes us stronger."
— **Friedrich Nietzsche**

October

Week 44   10/28/19 to 11/03/19

○ 28. MONDAY

PRIORITIES

○ 29. TUESDAY

○ 30. WEDNESDAY

TO DO

○ 31. THURSDAY

○ 1. FRIDAY

○ 2. SATURDAY / 3. SUNDAY

"For every minute you are angry you lose sixty seconds of happiness."
— **Ralph Waldo Emerson**

October

Week 44   10/28/19 to 11/03/19

○ 28. MONDAY

PRIORITIES

○ 29. TUESDAY

○ 30. WEDNESDAY

TO DO

○ 31. THURSDAY

○ 1. FRIDAY

○ 2. SATURDAY / 3. SUNDAY

"Being deeply loved by someone gives you strength, while loving someone deeply gives you courage."
— **Lao Tzu**

November

Week 45   11/04/19 to 11/10/19

○ 4. MONDAY

                                                  PRIORITIES

○ 5. TUESDAY

○ 6. WEDNESDAY

                                                  TO DO

○ 7. THURSDAY

○ 8. FRIDAY

○ 9. SATURDAY / 10. SUNDAY

"If you can't explain it to a six year old, you don't understand it yourself."
— **Albert Einstein**

November

Week 45　　　　　　　　　　　　　11/04/19 to 11/10/19

○ 4. MONDAY

○ 5. TUESDAY

○ 6. WEDNESDAY

○ 7. THURSDAY

○ 8. FRIDAY

○ 9. SATURDAY / 10. SUNDAY

PRIORITIES

TO DO

"I'm not upset that you lied to me, I'm upset that from now on I can't believe you."
— **Friedrich Nietzsche**

November

Week 46

11/11/19 to 11/17/19

○ 11. MONDAY

PRIORITIES

○ 12. TUESDAY

○ 13. WEDNESDAY

TO DO

○ 14. THURSDAY

○ 15. FRIDAY

○ 16. SATURDAY / 17. SUNDAY

"If you want your children to be intelligent, read them fairy tales. If you want them to be more intelligent, read them more fairy tales."
— **Albert Einstein**

November

Week 47

11/18/19 to 11/24/19

○ 18. MONDAY

PRIORITIES

○ 19. TUESDAY

○ 20. WEDNESDAY

TO DO

○ 21. THURSDAY

○ 22. FRIDAY

○ 23. SATURDAY / 24. SUNDAY

"Folks are usually about as happy as they make their minds up to be."
— **Abraham Lincoln**

November

Week 48   11/25/19 to 12/01/19

○ 25. MONDAY

○ 26. TUESDAY

○ 27. WEDNESDAY

○ 28. THURSDAY

○ 29. FRIDAY

○ 30. SATURDAY / 1. SUNDAY

PRIORITIES

TO DO

"Logic will get you from A to Z; imagination will get you everywhere."
— **Albert Einstein**

December

Week 49

12/02/19 to 12/08/19

○ 2. MONDAY

○ 3. TUESDAY

○ 4. WEDNESDAY

○ 5. THURSDAY

○ 6. FRIDAY

○ 7. SATURDAY / 8. SUNDAY

PRIORITIES

TO DO

"The difference between genius and stupidity is: genius has its limits."
— **Alexandre Dumas-fils**

December

Week 50

12/09/19 to 12/15/19

○ 9. MONDAY

PRIORITIES

○ 10. TUESDAY

○ 11. WEDNESDAY

TO DO

○ 12. THURSDAY

○ 13. FRIDAY

○ 14. SATURDAY / 15. SUNDAY

"'Classic' - a book which people praise and don't read."
— **Mark Twain**

December

Week 51   12/16/19 to 12/22/19

○ 16. MONDAY

PRIORITIES

○ 17. TUESDAY

○ 18. WEDNESDAY

TO DO

○ 19. THURSDAY

○ 20. FRIDAY

○ 21. SATURDAY / 22. SUNDAY

"Go to heaven for the climate and hell for the company."
— **Benjamin Franklin Wade**

December

Week 52   12/23/19 to 12/29/19

○ 23. MONDAY

                                           PRIORITIES

○ 24. TUESDAY

○ 25. WEDNESDAY

                                           TO DO

○ 26. THURSDAY

○ 27. FRIDAY

○ 28. SATURDAY / 29. SUNDAY

"If I had a flower for every time I thought of you...I could walk through my garden forever."
— **Alfred Tennyson**

December

Week 1   12/30/19 to 01/05/20

○ 30. MONDAY

PRIORITIES

○ 31. TUESDAY

○ 1. WEDNESDAY

TO DO

○ 2. THURSDAY

○ 3. FRIDAY

○ 4. SATURDAY / 5. SUNDAY

"Life is like riding a bicycle. To keep your balance, you must keep moving."
— **Albert Einstein**

NAME	TELEPHONE NUMBER

NAME	TELEPHONE NUMBER

NAME	TELEPHONE NUMBER

NAME	TELEPHONE NUMBER

www.ingramcontent.com/pod-product-compliance
Lightning Source LLC
Chambersburg PA
CBHW081603220526
45468CB00010B/2748